Where We Let Go

poems by

Cindy Kelly Benabderrahman

Finishing Line Press
Georgetown, Kentucky

Where We Let Go

Copyright © 2019 by Cindy Kelly Benabderrahman
ISBN 978-1-63534-916-0 First Edition
All rights reserved under International and Pan-American Copyright Conventions.
No part of this book may be reproduced in any manner whatsoever without written permission from the publisher, except in the case of brief quotations embodied in critical articles and reviews.

ACKNOWLEDGMENTS

Grateful acknowledgement to the following journals, in which these poems were previously published:

"In Cedar" in *Panamowa*
"Rich People" in *Orange Room Review*
"A Record of Things" in *Hiss Quarterly*
"Pageantry" in *Red Eft Review*

Publisher: Leah Maines
Editor: Christen Kincaid
Cover Art: *Celestial Beings* by Erin S. Mader
Author Photo: George M. Donaldson
Cover Design: Cindy Kelly Benabderrahman

Printed in the USA on acid-free paper.
Order online: www.finishinglinepress.com
also available on amazon.com

Author inquiries and mail orders:
Finishing Line Press
P. O. Box 1626
Georgetown, Kentucky 40324
U. S. A.

Table of Contents

A Record of Things 1

Reading Jimmy Carter's Memoir 2

We Ordered our Prints through the Mail 4

Separation 6

Rich People 9

In the Children's Choir at the Amsterdam Church of God 10

The Living Room 12

Changeling 13

In Cedar 16

An Elegy 20

Porches 21

For Good 22

Pageantry 24

This is my grief hair 25

The Feast 26

Almost Mother's Day 28

*To Jenn Bash,
for getting it,
for being the light,*

*and for Drake Kelly,
who reminds me.*

*In memory of my mother,
Cathy Jean Kelly,
whose vivid joy filled my world.*

A Record of Things

Peeling stories off the wall
paper, in layers, in ribbons
of how tall Cathy Jean was
on her different birthdays,
(remember the year
Kate iced the cake
with the –ay in *birthday*
and the –an in *Jean* scrunched
up a little too close to the rainbow
of roses).

It peels off in reminders
of who got in trouble
for coloring on the wall,
that kid kind of cave art:
clumsy circles, a school
of jellyfish, roosters, maudlin
shapes that, like summer clouds,
transform into what we want them to.

Under the paper live stains
and bumps, little valleys
and ridges where cats scratched,
dents where door knobs scarred,
and those bright places
where pictures of family
reunions and portraits of a girl
with the prettiest smile
hung like loyal defenders
of pea-green paisley,
of pears and roosters,
of gold filigree.

Reading Jimmy Carter's Memoir

How, how, how is President Carter ninety
years old, when I swear I'm still riding on the floor,
wandering in and out of present tense and past,
in the back seat of my grandparents' Plymouth
Gran Fury. The vinyl seats are too hot, and they burn
the backs of my thighs because it's 1980,
and these velour shorts are short.
It's Sunday, and we're going visiting
to my grandparents' friends, Mary and Roy.

Their place always smelled of fresh-cut hay,
that smell got down real deep in my lungs;
we ran and ran and the tall grass stung
our legs, and it hurt catching our breath—
me and their grandkids—I never remembered
their names, but we had the grandest picnics
on enormous quilts, and then we'd lay in the grass and watch
the sky, bellies full of sloppy joes and Mountain Dews and potato
salad, drowsy as the sun got low in the orange sky.

Our grandparents played euchre, talked in serious tones
about President Carter and the UMWA, about farming
and the economy, and the Soviets, what we had canned,
what we still had to freeze before the frost.

I always fell asleep across the back seat on the way home.
Someone carried me in and I'd wake up sunburnt
in a house that smelled like apple dumplings, my
grandmother complaining that the U.S. was boycotting
the summer Olympics and something or other was happening
with the UMWA insurance.

Carter moved out, and Reagan moved in,
and I am still riding around with my mother
in her Oldsmobile station wagon with wood grain trim,
picking up Tupperware in Pittsburgh, business as usual,

and one day, for fifteen minutes, we joined six-point-five million people
holding hands across America.

Life is like that. You wake up one day, and the Berlin
Wall comes down. Years later, people are selling bits and pieces
of it on eBay, and National Geographic has more followers
on Instagram than it does readers of its print magazine.

I'm thirty-seven, and Jimmy Carter is not the President.
He is Ninety. Years. Old.
My grandparents are gone.
My mother is gone. And I'm married
to this Algerian man who is reading a newspaper—
in French, online, in my living room,
my grandparents' wood-paneled living room,
while their newspaper clippings are taped
in a rainbow of yellowed layers to the insides
of the cupboard doors in the kitchen
and I realize that everything that ever happened
is still happening all at once,

that even though my husband and my mother
never stood in the same room,
I'm still waking up every morning
wearing my Princess Leia underoos,
and they're both of them right here
in all kinds of vivid technicolor
beside me.

We Ordered our Prints through the Mail

Moments take the shapes of rectangles;
in their geographies, we are still
together, I'm still small
enough to sleep on my grandmother's lap,
her big, careful hands smooth my tangled hair
from my forehead. In this one, my brother
has crawled up into our chair, and we doze together,
underexposed. Here, fingers learn to crochet,
to bang out a Sonatina on the Wurlitzer.

In that one, my mother has just turned nineteen,
a piece of candy in her hand. In that one a kiss,
an awkward attempt at a Viennese Waltz,
the Twist, a first broken bone.

This is what's left now:
Faces that sing, silent with unmoving lips
in the shapes of Os, making a choir
of smiles and salt and family get-togethers,
of tapioca pudding and homemade birthday
cakes. We made a moment out of every gift
ever unwrapped in this kitchen with its pine
walls, this living room with brown, threadbare
wall-to-wall carpeting.

The textures are flat, though, and do not come close
to translating how I still know, in fleeting
moments, exactly what the ridges feel like in the pattern
of paisley on those vinyl kitchen chairs, the sticky way clothes
cling to our bodies, drenched in the gritty, tomatoey sweat
of canning day, what it smells like to snap fresh green beans.
I still know the cool, damp grit of garden dirt and gravel
under my bare feet and the tart bite of a fresh radish,
rubbed almost clean with my grandfather's tee shirt. I still hear
the sharp whipping wind snapping fresh wet sheets
hung out to dry, the cool of the shade underneath
a maple tree long dead now, the pinch of nylon belts
in the seats of long-gone lawn chairs. I know
the smooth of my grandmother's thumbnail, the tenor
of my grandfather's young voice, the vibrating handle
of the pitchfork tining for nightcrawlers,
the sharp taste of a mouthful of fresh-caught bluegill
fried in homemade batter, the simple joy of singing along
with the AM radio in my grandfather's Valiant,
thinking it would last forever.

Separation

In that place between where we hold
on and where we let go, we are still touching
there, my hand in your hand, my hand still
small, now your hand in mine—your papery, wrinkly, love
worn, beautiful bony hand. We're inside that place
where there's a quiet, cool breath going to come between us
any time now, then that cold, frantic ache'll settle in
to our bones—the same one I had when I woke up
sleep-sweating as a kid, when for crying out loud,
you'd untangle me from the blankets, ease me out
into your arms, that easy, just-a-nightmare-it'll-be-alright,
don't-wake-your-grandmother-up, let's-go-out-in-the-kitchen-
and-share-a mayonnaise-sandwich feeling
and I want to feel it now, but this time you're completely gone.

I can't shake this guilty place, this regret
for not paying more attention to the grace
with which you'd slice an onion thinner than paper
using the penknife you kept in your overhauls,
the eloquence of your proud-of-me wrinkles, laughter
in your wide-open eyes every day when you asked me
did I think Xzibit and Mad Mike
would want to pimp that old sky blue 1987 Chevy
farm truck we used to share after my car broke down,
and now I'm here, standing where you left
me at the edge of this new world
without you.

You're not here to tell me what's wrong
with the movies, how nobody in his son-of-a-bitching right
mind woulda give all the ammunition to the idiot
in Saving Private Ryan, how you were at Remagen;
how it really went down was nothing of the sort.
You're not here to segue into how you got away
from the Germans that time you and a buncha guys were separated
from the rest of your battalion and all you had was the mess

truck. And yet, I close my eyes and you still take me with you
down those dotted lines on the 656 Tank Destroyer Battalion map
in your Army yearbook, I can still hear you telling me all about
spreading out all the tin cups and plates and pans behind you
on the road as you fled, placing landmines under some of them
so they had to stop and check each one, and how, when you met
back up with the rest of the battalion, they were mad because you lost
all the kitchen stuff.

That would make a much better story, you tell me,
not like these slow shows. You remained optimistic
about Flags of Our Fathers, said we'd go together
so long as you didn't come out of that hospital on a slab.

We never saw that film together.
I can't bear to watch it alone, and the fringed sun
I used to draw in grade school is settling down
behind this huge, lonesome horizon.

Here, at the beginning of spring, there are hailstones;
handfuls of gravel sifting through my fingers
where in that long-off childhood, a train whistle
blows, a little girl is baiting her first hook,
catching her first bluegill.

I carry the photograph you carried
in your wallet for thirty years, scratched
from every time you loved me and my mom
and my brother enough to slide it out of your wallet,
show it off to someone you hadn't seen in ages.

I can't help but feel a sense of loss: stories
I will never know, know-how, where things belong,
how to put things together that I will never understand
because they've gone with you.

This dream I keep having about finding you
again in the place at end of the world,
now more than ever and with a sense of urgency
I've never known before in my adult life,
I need it to come true.

Rich People

The last time we drove to the bank
in Bergholz, we passed
the white salt box house
on the curve before the tracks,
and you laughed and laughed
and said you thought the people
who lived in that house were rich
when you were a little kid
because they had pillars
on the front of their house
holding up the porch roof.

When I drive by there now,
the bluish light from their television
flickers through their windows
and I imagine them in there
eating popcorn together,
knowing nothing of my grief,
richer than ever.

In the Children's Choir at the Amsterdam Church of God

we didn't know anything
about the human condition,
just a hall full of umbrellas
and raincoats

our mouths open wide
in joyful songs about love
in any language, maybe
the language of birds—
like remarkable wrens,
we shall not be moved

we sounded like owls
through a stove pipe;
we hooped and we hollered
in the churchyard
where that lucky tornado
sat down the steeple years ago
to make room for the new one

we channeled
our animal grandmothers:
we sang all the songs
of peculiar angels,
lifted our off-key voices
full of gladsome joy
with all the grace
of unhatched eggs

glory glory glory
and in between the alleluias,
we thought about the carnival
in Bergholz, the odd dischord
of the barrel organ in the carousel

and behind our song, I recognized
those maudlin evening screams
that reassured, but also
scared the living daylights
right out of me.

The Living Room

Cocoon of cotton blankets nestled into October
between metal like honeycomb,
this room a living hive, you among them,

that swarm of people come to hold you
in a circle of hands with prayer and song,
teddy bears, a porcelain angel lumiere,
a painting of your grandson,
a Christmas tree, a wedding,
a violin song.

What else was in this room?
Your misunderstood desire to go outside,
a window opening, and beyond its frame,
someone only you could see.

I monitored the buzz of this room,
comings and goings, relatives, friends,
vultures, gawkers passing through.

When it was finally quiet,
you asked for wedding soup,
then Mountain Dew.
A final moment of clarity
that left you exhausted.

The landscape of your chest
heaved under your fifteen breaths
per minute, then twelve; I found myself
acutely aware that I had never existed
outside the rhythm of you,

that tomorrow
would bring one less constant
in my diminishing world.

Changeling

I am eight.
I am eight years old
and I am lying on my stomach
on the living room floor
in front of our cabinet
television set. It is seven a.m.
and I am watching *Flintstones*
then *Shirt Tales* then *Smurfs*.

It is 1983. Bo and Luke Duke ran off
to drive NASCAR, and to Boss Hog's chagrin,
Coy and Vance are riding around
in the General Lee,
jumping over creeks and screaming and yelling;
we are screaming and yelling,
our shorts are as short as Daisy's.

My brother is playing with his He-Man action figures
and his cardboard boxes and yarn.
My grandpa's Aunt Mary Marcus is still alive,
my grandmother is still alive. They are arguing
right now about what my Aunt Mary did with her dentures,
but we all know what she did with her dentures
because my grandfather has fished them out of the toilet
a hundred times.

My brother is tying his string around his He-Man
action figures and I have taken Evil-Lyn again.
I like her yellow legs and her small, hard body,
and I wish I were more like her.

My brother jumps
off the couch onto my back.
We don't know about his mental illness yet.
It is 1983, and his brain is not yet damaged.
My back is bruising.

There is his maniacal laughter.
When I try to wrench away,
he tears the sleeve
of my Return of the Jedi nightgown.

My brother is wearing his cowboy vest
and his cap gun holsters. He tells me he is *the law*.

My brother is making Prince Adam ride Battle Cat.
My brother is making He-Man ride Cringer.
My brother twisted my arm
and wrenched Evil-Lyn from my fist.
My brother is making Evil-Lyn ride Prince Adam.
My brother is making Evil-Lyn ride He-Man.
My brother is making Evil-Lyn ride Battle Cat.

It is 1997, and I am working summer theatre,
and I meet a girl with golden hair
whose voice was the voice of She-Ra.

It is 1985, and my brother is not allowed to play
with my She-Ra dolls, for the honor of Greyskull or not.

My mother doesn't know
my brother was switched
and I don't know
if it was for his evil designs
or his beauty or his platinum hair,
but he was somebody's exchange,
of this I am certain, but I keep it to myself.

Now my brother has forgotten his origin,
forgotten he is more goblin
than human, and nobody understands
why his behavior became uglier
and uglier, blaming it on psychology
and brain damage, drugs,
other things common to the human condition.

He survives,
this stock, he survives
and survives and survives.

It is 1987, and we are in the kitchen,
I have cooked my brother a meal
of eggs and bacon bits. I served it to him
in an egg shell in an egg cup.

He looks at me,
I fully expect him to confess
his crimes, but he just laughs
and laughs
and laughs

In Cedar

We keep our traditions packed away:
old suitcases, pillowcases, clothes,
out of vogue now, folded in neat stacks.
Feed-sack dishcloths,
aprons and Sunday gloves, afghans
and rain bonnets, quilt squares,
good scissors, unfinished crochet.

I remember this wallpaper:
a toille of fruit and farm birds,
this pine paneling:
its tongue, its groove,
these kitchen cupboards:
their maple, their shine,
white formica countertop,
gold flecks and all.

Our fruit cellar remembers being a coal cellar
once. She had her own door right there,
behind pickle barrels, fishing buckets.
There is a distinct memory here of black gold
by the shovel full, never empty.

They fished, we canned, us girls:
me and Grandma and my Great Aunt
Mary Davis boiled tomatoes,
pushed them through the sieve,
hot seeds and all.

When my grandmother smiled,
she looked young like my mom,
and I'm reminded that she fell
off a swing when she was just a girl my age,
and knocked out all her front teeth,
one just half grown in from the good set.

She wiped the sweat from her forehead
and smiled, her one false tooth yellowed,
cheeks steamed red.

She worked hard, made sure
we had tomato juice, pickled beets,
green beans, strawberry jam
to last all winter and then some.

This house is quiet, its two deep freezes
four bedrooms, clutter closets,
junk drawers, two cedar chests.
A million little hiding places
for tucking away and forgetting about.

These are the paper dolls we hung
in the door frames one New Years,
paper snowflakes from some long-ago
winter when I was still small enough
to cut this horribly, badly, perfectly.

The things we can't let go of
wait in piles, all lined up
like a little slumber party.
My kid teeth, aunt Goldie's braid,
real-feather pillows, decades
of Valentines, my Grandma's prosthesis,
her false tooth, her cancer
turbans, glasses.

We sang along with our ancestors,
their babies, moms and fathers,
remembered their memories
in glimpses of ours: almost-familiar
octogenarians admired my snow angels,

smiled out from photographs in which doors
lead to other rooms where a woman
who only exists now as a fraction of me
still hand-quilts patchwork,
embroiders the year on,
eighteen and seventy-one.

We waited for the first frost every year,
ready with cardboard and bailing twine,
waited for the fresh smell of the first snow,
for the egg timer to buzz pin curls dry,
we played solitaire, we didn't cheat,
and if we were lucky,
maybe every third time we won.

I remember this bedroom in layers:
sunlight filtered through in treescapes,
branches printed on the bedspreads.

We colored eggs with wax and vinegar
and food color, planted flowers at the graveyard,
put our hands over our star-spangled hearts.

Here are my grandmother's chenille blankets
and percale sheets, still fresh from hanging
on the line late 80s, smelling of nothing
but sunshine and cedar. If I look hard
I can see the creases where she made
the same hospital corners every day.

I'm overwhelmed; I don't keep up.
I pile mattresses two-deep
right on the floor and I lie here
reading my favorite novels over and over.

I wash my store-bought Ragu
down with Diet Pepsi. I never think
about the canning or the wash
or what's tucked away in cedar chests.

I let somebody else devil the eggs,
fill in the recipe books,
clip obituaries from the Herald Star
and the Free Press Standard.
I remember, but I do not continue.

I sneak cigarettes on the back porch,
I don't let the cat out. I watch my brother
mow the grass, think about pulling weeds
and planting onions and cabbages.
Maybe next year.

I think sometimes how things survive,
wonder what things didn't.
When my sins are counted,
what will be kept
of my left-behinds,
what will they add to the pile
with the remnants of the rest
who went before.

It's not the same since the world sped up;
there's no time to stop and make homemade
potato chips, potato candy,
perfect pie crusts, pizzelles,
or kielbasa and potato soup
with rivulets.

An Elegy

I always told you
I did not want a child,
but you knew the man
I'm going to marry

he has those dark wise eyes
of a wonderful father
and remember,
you said he had a kindness

in his voice
that made you smile, you said
you loved the way he talked
to me.

Right now I want nothing more
than to pick up an infant
the size of a doll,

to tell her
your grandmother
would have just loved you
to pieces.

Porches

My mother newly-widowed,
her friends tried to fix her up
on blind dates with good guys
and nice guys they knew;
she always declined
with grace.

Linda said she'd never meet
a good man if she waited for him
to show up on the front porch.

I was eight years old when Paul
arrived—he stumbled acrost the road
drunk from the Village Inn and sat
down on the back porch
swing next to Aunt Mary,
who pursed her lips
and made the Morgan face
that signaled aggravation.

My mother was making popcorn balls
with Red Hots when the phone rang,
a brief conversation in which
she twisted herself up
in the spiral of the telephone cord,
agreed to a first date.

When she died, I read her journal
where she wrote
the trouble with Linda
is she didn't know
which porch to look on.

For Good

Some days I wallow around
in what's left of you:
slips of paper I find
with your handwriting,
little things I know you loved

There are two reasons to keep things:
one is for good
the other in case

Grandma kept her china for good,
only to be used on special occasions.
Other stuff she packed away
for someday when you need it

like when you broke your tooth off
eating dinner at Panera Bread,
the same tooth absent from her smile
now absent from yours.

I found you in the kitchen
at midnight,
trying to wear her partial,
the bag in which it was packed away
dumped out on the counter—
her prosthetic breast,
her glasses

She kept secrets, too:
a lump she never mentioned
until it was too late.
You both died
before good ever got here.

Now we use the china
for everyday plates,
and we're paring down.

I only keep the important things:
memories of staying up late
reading David Sedaris
aloud to each other,
giggling when neither of us
could sleep.

Pageantry

In second grade,
my mother and her best friend
Rebecca took the shortcut
home from grade school,
fashioned a beauty pageant
from ribbons and flowers
they found in the trash out back
of Sweeney-Dodd's funeral home.

"In Memoriam" and "Dear Husband"
sashayed home with lily-scented hair,
their pageant sashes sparkling with glitter.

This is my grief hair

sticking out everywhere
please do not poke fun
of its knots and tangles
or the way it's flattened
itself out against my pillow
late at night.

it's trying to cope
with the way I've been
mistreating it,
the dirt and grime
and oil it's collected
as I've neglected
it these weeks
that have passed
since my mother
passed away,

in which I realized
that clean, shiny hair
is not important,
that mourning hair
looks a lot
like morning hair.

The Feast

The very young do not know
grief; they are unaffected
joy. They love, accept love;
they do not try
to understand it.

Then comes the day.
It sneaks up
and sits right in your chair,
takes your place
at the kids' table,
invites itself to your feast.
Welcome to it.

Eat up,
an amuse bouche—
(I was five years old when my father
was murdered on Venice Beach)—
a heartache garnished
with the deep, ink-black caviar
of grief.

Eventually, you're served
the tasting menu—
you're seated at the chef's table
for the prix fixe;
when you've finished the dessert
course, you lick that plate
clean, sop up all that sorrow
and get a mouth-feel
for the bittersweet,
your very own Vanitas.

Only you can't really say
how it is; you cannot describe its reach.
People tell you:
it gets easier
or it takes time,

you know those comforts
are empty promises;
those folks must not have been
as glued together
to the ones they lost
somehow.

I certainly can't explain it
to my five-year-old nephew,
who has just lost his Grammy.
I can't tell him about the deep-down
of the chasm inside when he asks,
why you crying Aunt Ninny?

I can't tell my mother,
I know now. I know
what you meant
when you said I'd understand
when you were gone.

I can't ask the people
who knew this grief before me,
How did you do this alone?

All I can do is love
the ones I have left
and pray I have what it takes
to keep them away from the edge
of that big, black gaping gorge
as long as humanly possible.

Almost Mother's Day

I'm in these photographs; the late seventies, the early eighties
seem like silhouettes, sunsets, overcast with milk and butter
and sunshine; there's a warmth there, frosted in daylight,
an uncertain glare not unlike squinting my eyes looking out
the window of my grandpa's old Valiant, right into the sun,
the warmth of acoustic guitars, eight tracks, and am radios,
the warmth of my favorite Tigers sweatshirt, of fire, people
holding hands just off the frame of the picture, the parts
of the photo I remember in my mind—there are children
with flowers in their hair and waterfalls, long legs, old ladies
smiling on porch swings, a tiny yellow church, a picnic,
a shade tree, daydreams.

Setting: Maybe 1983. Rainbows were just rainbows.
There is a swarm of Girl Scouts in a field
throwing hundreds of dandelions into the air.

The sun catches your face. I imagine
your face from the perspective of the sun
and I fall in love.

I fancy you moving at the speed of light
beneath canopies you conjure, framing out
a shelter house to protect it all the way you want for me
to remember:

blissful days, cool wind on my sunburns, us around a bonfire
at night, the blackened goo of a marshmallow, the char
of a hickory stick, finding the shadow of God's grace
wherever we were together.
And this is what you taught me:

Faith follows Faith.
>There is a moment
>in which every trapeze artist
>must let go
>so the next one can catch her.
>That moment is long enough for lifetimes.

Love follows Love.

Everywhere I look, there is something beautiful:
Milkweed, Queen Anne's Lace, the sunburn
peeling from your freckled back, the henna flowers
on my hands, collecting the pieces of paper I find
folded up with your handwriting.

And now:
My husband's espresso-
tobacco breath,
buildings in my mind,
places we will live
together, a future sewn
together with needles
carved from bone,
eighty-eight piano keys,
a hungry lark.

And still,
this is the worst kind of loneliness I've ever known:
Being unable to talk to you.

Everywhere I go, I'm by myself.

Cindy Kelly Benabderrahman lives in Amsterdam, Ohio in a mid-nineteenth century American Pyramidal house originally built as housing for the coal mine that once operated across the railroad tracks. She shares her home with her Algerian husband, Oualid, who received his American citizenship on Valentine's Day, 2018. He arrived in the US with only a suitcase; now they share this house and its three generations of left-behinds.

Cindy is also a mixed media artist and photographer, and her work is sometimes shown at the Salt Kettle Gallery in Salineville, Ohio or in her sporadically-stocked Etsy shop. She spends a lot of her spare time researching her Melungeon ancestry. She is the Director of Community Outreach for The St. Gertrude Cat Initiative, and she is also currently serving as Secretary for Ohio members of Modern Woodmen Fraternal Financial.

From 2007-2012, Cindy was the editor of *Plain Spoke*, the literary speakeasy journal at Amsterdam Press, where she also edited the Gob Pile Chapbook Series.

Her writing is informed by place, family, friendship, faith, and grief. Her life has been staccatoed by loss, but she still delights in the odd and wonderful joys of being a wife and an aunt.

She loves travel and adventure, and she's happiest exploring old and ancient, out of the way places. She has a habit of doing things on the spur of the moment. She feels at home in river cities like Pittsburgh with its hundreds of bridges. She loves West Virginia, too, that mountain mama, and yet, the first time she saw New York City, it felt like home.

She and her husband were married in the winding, maze-like casbah of Tunis, Tunisia; she wore a white dress and gold slippers, and a silk Kate Spade scarf embellished with orange camels and pom pom fringe. No matter where she travels, though, she returns to Appalachia again and again.

She holds a Master of Science in Reading/Education from Franciscan University of Steubenville and a Bachelor of Arts in English with The Writing Minor from Kent State University.

For several years, Cindy taught English Comp I and II, Journalism, and Remedial English at Eastern Gateway Community College. She enjoyed the challenge of working with displaced coal miners and steelworkers who populated her classes; they taught her as much as she taught them. She also taught 11th grade American Literature, Grammar, and Mythology at an Ohio public online school. She left education to work with her stepbrother and sister-in-law, whose company builds and maintains communication towers. She's also a part-time freelance writer.

Some of her favorite writers are Maurice Sendak, Gabriel Garcia Marquez, L. Frank Baum, Madeleine L'Engle, and Billy Collins. She loves Wes Anderson films and post rock, and she gets nostalgic about star-shaped sunglasses and growing up in the 1980s.

She's been a lifelong fan of Princess Leia.

www.ingramcontent.com/pod-product-compliance
Lightning Source LLC
LaVergne TN
LVHW040117080426
835507LV00041B/1335